Songs The Moon Sings

By
Michael C. Owens

© 2019 Michael C. Owens. All rights reserved.
ISBN 978-0-9838021-2-9

Previous works by Michael C. Owens

- **Desert Well and Other Poems**
- **Stained Glass** - Meditations on Faith

This volume, and his other publications, can be ordered via the author's online page hosted by Lulu.com (an online publisher) at **http://www.lulu.com/spotlight/mcowens**

The author's (vastly underused and only occasionally maintained) personal web page may be found at **http://www.mcowens.com**

Email (may or may not be responded to - <u>make sure</u> the subject line begins with the word "Book" or your email may be summarily consigned to the nether realms without even a glance):
mcowens@mcowens.com

Forward

It has been noted many times, by many people in the literary world, that in this day and age poetry is widely viewed as either trivial (think nursery rhymes ... which historically are usually not trivial at all, but then one must be something of a historian to know that), or too esoteric or *avant-garde* to be of interest to the average person. There is truth in both views, but there is also much poetry, and much in poetry, that can evoke a variety of positive and illuminating responses as well.

Perhaps some of the more insightful reasons given for shunning poetry, especially good poetry, is the need to set aside time, find a place with few distractions, and focus more closely on what the poet has written. Come to think about it, those are actually excellent reasons to read poetry. Nevertheless, in today's fast paced world, that equates to a lot of work, and the reader may not be particularly convinced the return on that time/place/focus effort will be worth it.

Then there is the need to think. For oneself. Sometimes abstractly. Now that is indeed a burden for most. Poems are often puzzles, sometimes allegorical, tend to use lots of metaphors, frequently compressing far reaching concepts into tightly woven webs of words. Of course, sometimes they are not abstruse at all and come across clearly and simply.

So here is a collection of poems in a variety of styles for your reading pleasure. Some are complex, some simple, some require looking up words and names, others ... well, see for yourself.

I thank you for your interest in poetry, and especially my poetry, and willingness to spend time and effort in untangling whatever mysteries may be found therein, and herein. Enjoy!

Michael C. Owens

Contents

FOREWORD 3
POETRY 7
   A Lady of Letters 9
   The Arc of Dawn 10
   Perspective 11
   Martyrdom 12
   Heralds Of Ragnarok 13
   Muse 16
   Okay God, Let's Talk 17
   On The Eve of Easter Sunday 18
   The Verdict 19
   The Ledge 20
   Air Superiority 21
   On Annie (after e. e. cummings) 22
   Memory's Shadow 23
   Fifteen Shells In A Box 24
   Wind 25
   Breathless 26
   Weaver 27
   Kent State, May 4, 1970 28
   Claim Jumper 29
   On Reading An Untitled Poem 30
   YHWH 32
   Orb 34
   An Invitation 35
   Summer Night 36
   Sendai, March 2011 37
   Sonata For Moonlight And Shadows 38

HAIKU 39
   A Comment on Haiku 40

POETRY

A Lady of Letters

I once knew a lady of letters,
who managed to cast off her fetters.
Her poems rhymed phrases
her prose brought her praises,
and soon she wore suede on her sweaters.

Five line Limerick.

The Arc of Dawn

"I'll sacrifice the lamb that I do love
To spite a raven's heart within a dove."
*   - Orsino, in Twelfth Night (Shakespeare)*

Imagine reality if you must - that regal
usurper, pretender to the throne of reason,
imperious proclaimer of edicts based solely on figments
of a probabilistic, fragmented universe termed facts;
those chimeras of contemplated observation,
mediated by memes, prisoners of percepts, veiled
in robes visible only to functionaries and fools.

So I, a dreamer, bound for the arc of dawn
that marks the shore of life's entropic sea,
exclaim, release a raven into the cosmos
to confound creation with thought and meaning
born from the embrace of fantasy and myth.
Dream ... a seductress who sheds her veils of reason
until just a whisper of her skin's perfume remains.

Passion and lust now dance, entrain reality,
skew the curves, erect new paradigms,
transform reason. Facts constrain, imprison,
slay prophets and changelings, kings, and dreamers.
Ah, but the dominatrix Desire enslaves
all in her presence. Facts are her vassals.
She beckons, and reality, and reason, succumb.

Perspective

A cloud hugged the moon this morning - in vain
of course. The moon, aloof and distant and pale,
asked the cloud, "but why? You have the sky,
the sun, the earth and wind with which to dance
and spin. My path is fixed and change is slow,
I ask for nothing, and yet you offer all."

"I understand," the cloud replied. "It's all
perspective, yet my warmth is real. Though slow,
my circling mists now glow within and dance
with your light a pas de deux, with all the sky
a stage, the wind soft symphony, and pale
dawn the curtain. Hope is never in vain."

Martyrdom

I turn my anger on the rising sun
and curse its bitter light, invasive warmth.
Such promise seems a vain attempt to sooth -
a remorseless taunt, corrupt and threatening.

Against this flight of thought I lift my fears
as shield of ignorance, encapsuled night,
banner of absolutes, unquestioned truths.
And if I could I would deny the sun.

Heralds of Ragnarok

This poem is not for you, sneering realist,
you without insight or dreams, locked within
your formal arcs of reason, main sequence
stars, and spectroscopic analyses.

Myths are myth, you decry, and fail
to see the shadow of entangling sophistry
lurking deep beneath your sine wave sea,
fail to hear the cantor's skirl, the wail

rising from the throes of death and birth,
calling forth the gods who formed this earth
then set it wheeling down destruction's path
to be riven by battle, drowned or risen anew.

The provenance of creation is fantastical sight,
blind to logic, the suspension of disbelief.
Wonder is feeling beyond the reach of reason.
Reason has no soul , no human touch

or embrace. The heart of love beats in shaded
realms rampant with satyrs and nymphs, fairies,
and great serpents pleasuring in darkling lochs.
Logic fails at a lover's glance or touch.

For just this side of morning there are dragons
with unfurled wings, scales, and bloody claws,
who sport with knights and maidens, changelings and kings,
quaff ale with ogres and trolls and booted cats.

The past, what was, is born in a minstrel's lay.
What will be, known only to oracles and seers.

What is, now lies precisely in between -
Salome's last veil, a gossamer wisp of nothing.

Just this side of morning the piquant taste
of a kiss thought stolen but then returned, eyes closed,
blinds lovers to logic, lifts them to clouds and rain.
Paeans rise to Apollo. Chaste Artemis departs.

Open your eyes, benighted bastards of reason.
You were born of myth and fantasy - Vedic, Greek,
Norse, and more. You nursed at Hera's breasts,
worshiped Eros, sacrificed to Tlaloc.

You, who pursue to disembowel creation,
to challenge the gods, remember Pierus' daughters.
You rape Sophia, sire the Demiurge,
pay him homage as sophists' high priest.

Exalting self you fail to hear a distant
howl, the bloody hound Garmr, approaching.
Imagine, if you can, the plain beyond
death - aglitter with your star formed ashes.

Percepts and memes and quantum mechanics rule
this whirling, probabilistic world we share
with Leprechauns and leptons. We are gods
born in a dark that stretches reason's reach,

yet there we find our reason, unbounded creation.
There we raise dreams from dust, to people a future.
There hear songs that mend our tattered souls,
sooth a child, or rouse a warrior's rage.

Magic leads reason a merry chase, laughing

as each spell is caught, only to cast another.
Entranced, we are drawn as a moth to the flame of myth,
as defiant Icarus, enthralled, to the sun.

This poem is not for you, bereft reason,
fearful of serpents at horizon's edge. It calls
to those who chase rainbows, ride dragons, brave the abyss,
and sound the gjallarhorn to herald Ragnarok.

Muse

"Write from your heart," she said,
Then touching my head, went on:
"To capture dawn's swift flight
Leave sloe-eyed night's deceits
And sweet conceits behind.
Seek life to find your art."

Six line iambic trimeter. A nod to Sir Philip Sidney (1554-1586), who wrote before I knew him. End words have internal rhymes in following line, and last word rhymes internally with first line - ab/bc/cd/de/ef/fa.

Okay God, Let's Talk

Okay, God, let's talk. I think it's time you spit it out, and gave it to us straight. It's sure not coming from your reps, those lukewarm, milquetoast, spineless priests who tremble in the pulpit, casting fearful glances at those pews that hold the purse strings holders.

And thanks just loads for all that writ the people call your 'Word' - ambiguous with hoary age, that some would say they understand, forgetting time, and place, and land. They claim the Book, if read just right, if read exactly right, excising all that doesn't fit into their nice, neat, niche - they claim the Book has answered all the questions ever asked, and by extension all the questions never asked, not then, not now, and never more to come.

I think it's fear - a frantic grasping after anything to keep their faith afloat - a desperate need for answers with foundations built on rock, above an ever churning sea of questions, doubts, and ambiguity.

Oh sure, we're godseed if you will, at least that is our claim, sown randomly across creation's untilled fields of promised pleasure-pain. Godseed - so many fallen on hard ground.

On the Eve of Easter Sunday

"A dollar for bus fare?" A voice rose from the side.
"Sir?" She asked, and hopefully cocked her head.
I shrugged and turned away, shook my head.
"Jesus," I thought, "whatever became of pride?"

The Verdict

She spoke as if it mattered. Shrill at first,
a widow's whine, but later resolute.
Unbending - persistent and annoying.
He had no need of her - a waste of time.
Her case was trite and common, profitless,
beneath his skill, as were they all, but still
she wouldn't go away, and he was tested.
A judge, adjudicating simple laws
in complex times, he sat above them all,
yet here she came again.
                              Enough. The day
grows short, its shadow worries the edge of night,
slips its leash, is lost.
                           The provenance of Justice
is guilt by gold, the bloodied edge of a sword,
a patron's pale nod where fate and faith cross.
Law is shaped by circumstance, a cause,
or narrow point of view. There is no right
that can't be wrong, no wrong that can't be right.
He saw no need to know the whole of it
or its merit. With appeasement comes relief,
is that not just? The matter was not what mattered,
nor means, nor ends but, he feared, not God nor Man.

The Ledge

I am serene
a fluffy cumulus puff
a fleecy gleaming
white ball wrapped in blue
adrift on heaven's
languid pond.

No. I am cold
a mare's tail
lofty sky broom
that sweeps crystal
across the sky -
icy portent.

Or towering threat -
a thunderhead
roiling and brooding
unstoppable dark purpose
a hurler of lightening
and cleansing rain.

A raindrop - yes!
I am a raindrop
hidden among clouds
unknown and silent
I jump and hurtle down
to find concrete eternity

Air Superiority

Wasp waisted fighter
With chattering sting
Screams

Originally written during the Vietnam war. Dusted off for Iraq. Seems to never get old.

on annie (after e.e. cummings)

I liked annie (who's
dad had)
sad too
bad she died
mad (better
had it been)
her dad

Memory's Shadow

I see shame in what I've left undone
and loudly blame time's remorseless flow
as though I were a child again, as though
my bitter wails and flailing thoughts might rouse
my god, might bring her warmth, encircling arms,
a soothing voice; and I could lay my fears
against her breasts, be calmed by gentle touch,
forgiving kiss, then sent to play again.

Tonight a winter storm drums the roof;
clouds of rain descend through veils of thought
to swell deep pools beside my outside walk,
and I recall a boyhood wooden boat
launched in bone chilled wonder from the curb,
no shore in sight, released to watch it go
and ride the passing flood without the weight
of age or helmsman, hindsight, map, or plan.

I brood so much on time - remorseless time
that holds my past as introspective proof
of what was done and what was left undone.
These shadows cast by memories are long
near close of day. The storms of past and present
erode the heights and flood the depths in passion's
ebb and flow. I search to find myself,
that boyhood wooden boat, and forgiving arms.

Fifteen Shells in a Box

How is it that shells this dull can brighten
my day already filled with unshadowed sun?
Perhaps the gift is just a gift, without
pretense or meaning - simply that and nothing
more. Yet in the stillness of my thoughts,

awash and lost on Western Senegal's beach,
I take a moment's mindful stroll and find
in the simplicity of the whole of water,
beach worn shells, and sunshine, a mindful gift,
and I accept with silent, thoughtful, thanks.

Wind

Don't tell me God's humor has run out -
just now a cardinal, with aplomb, dodged
a palm's swaying fronds as if to flout
the blustery wind. He could have gone around;
instead he charged the gauntlet, a blurred shout,
then perched on the fence as if to say "there,
ample demonstration for you who doubt."

Breathless

hard surging pulsing chords that swirl
throbbing beat of rhythm's heat
sink and soar and float and dive
through streaming shafts of hot and blue
paisley notes of hue and cry
curl and twist in glowing tones
like restless waves that crest and lap
on heaven's deep and misty shore
until a blast of bright so white
that stunned the dazzled chords take flight
to surge and fling and shout about
then down in dissonant jarring bounce
from beat to beat then softly sound
to depths of earth's warm central tone
that pulses, pushes, penetrates
each broken note and surges through
each broken chord until again
arise a song but changed to find
new patterns beats new heights new depths
in swirling surging pulsing heat

Weaver

My youth filled frenzied flight
tripped your silken trap.
Caught in your web of words,
in threads drawn from life,
my entanglement came with struggle
and your bite was felt but faintly.
The fire now drawn from within
a cool peace comes
like mists down the mountains
that veil the greens and browns,
turning the world to gray.
The air heralds dusk,
suspending all in nothing.
My empty husk now cold,
the roots of the mountains are still.

Kent State, May 4, 1970

my thoughts clutch at feathers
cat killed dove down
drifts to my door
silent light and gray
like the death
of a dream

Claim Jumper

I claim the seas, all depths and reach at hand,
their shapes as kissed by wind and cupped by land,
the waves that stroke dark rocks or charge the sand,
the tides that rise or fall at pale moon's command.

I claim the hues and scents of growing things,
the scratch of bark, the gloss of dragon wings,
and tastes both sweet and bitter, the pixie rings
in dark green glens from which the priestess sings.

I claim the dappled, noon draped trees, and bright
rayed clouds as summer sets, the arching starlight
that spins and dances on a chill winter night,
and silver dawns first met by dreams' last flight.

I claim the sigh of winds, an angry rain,
whispers, laughter, cries of pleasure or pain,
a critic's harsh rasp and a lover's soft refrain,
the newborn's cry, a rustling page, your name.

I claim each sliver of sunlight, the rainbow's arc,
the cool dews of morning, a campfire's spark,
this susurrus pen as my thoughts find their mark,
your scent as you pass, the pause and jump of my heart.

On Reading an Untitled Poem

It's rare that I can find the time I need, or quiet space, to sit and read a poem. This morning though, I rose before a choir of birds called up the sun, and thus found both. So, sitting comfortably, computer at the fore, with coffee handy on the right, at left a day old scone, among the piles of "urgent" papers strewn around, I read.

With elbow planted on the desk, an ink stained thumb supporting chin, my index finger laid across pursed lips, I slow to catch the fullness of the poet's tack and craft. Behind and far above, a wind pressed cloud reluctantly decides to let the morning pass. An old discarded metal frame is tipped against the redwood fence outside my window, playing catch with the light - a muted, mirror glow that nags the eye, not blinding but distracting, chasing diffused thoughts.

If life can be defined by stone it will be found in jade, a gauzy mirror of the past and gateway to the soul. There's fire in opal, ruby glows, and emerald soothes, but life is lacking - cold, remote. In jade one sinks into the blue-green depths of storied bamboo forests, marks their creaking shafts and feels the exhaled mountain mists descending watercolor slopes. Translucent jade holds life's bare essence - living water, swirling air - surrounding fragile paper skies, and muted dripping from the tips of slender leaves. Whatever else jade is, the mind creates, and there finds peace and closure.

And here the poet finds a warrior, cloaked in jade. Such art, such honor, draped across a man of war. And yet it should not seem so strange, as over time all craft yields art. This warrior, master of his craft, knew war as more than killing skills, though art is found in that as well. A ruler of another age once wrote that war was too significant to be decided by the sword.

Oh, strength of arm prevails, when force is met by force. But war is done and victory is final in the mind, not on the field - not with defeat of arms, but through a change of heart. Who then has won? Such art requires neither sword nor shield, no armor, but a master's skill, attention, touch - applied with understanding, diligence, respect and love for self, the enemy, and stone.

The poet, artist, and the warrior, join together on this field once littered with stilled shards of life; and gathered up, the stones are shaped - rectangles - polished, set in order - jade to hold an image of the past in misty hues and tones, words to honor these remains, the warrior and the artist.

We turn and leave the close pressed air of silent vaults, and step outside into the past. Oh yes, it's here, in ancient yellow dust below immortal skies - endless children, practicing the crafts of war, their sunlit battle kites of blue-green silken cloth, rectangles strewn across the living breeze.

What honor, what reward, will crown the best of these? Perhaps, as in the past, a rectangle of jade.

The poet doesn't say.

YHWH

He rose and brushed a hand across his robe,
to loose the clinging courtyard dust,
a dust the unnamed raised,
then turned again to face the restive crowd.
He held the moment, sighed and spoke
to show how they were made.

The woman stood disheveled, caught and bound
by rigid temple law, condemned -
a sin. The snare was set,
and slipped - judge first yourselves, he ruled, then her.
He bent to touch the dust again,
to free its form, to write.

Two six line stanzas, iambic blank verse.
Leviticus 20:10: "The man who commits adultery with another man's wife, even he who commits adultery with his neighbor's wife, the adulterer and the adulteress shall surely be put to death." It is useful to note that only the woman was brought before Jesus.
From James McBride, http://www.abcog.org/nh/name.htm : "It was in the early Hellenistic period [shortly before the time of Jesus], following the translation of the Scriptures into Greek, that the Jews began to follow the Gentile mystical practice of attributing to God an "unutterable name of the divine essence". The Jews, to avoid any possibility of going contrary to Leviticus 24:16, had a superstitious regard for the name of God, both in speaking and writing."
Leviticus 24:16: "He who blasphemes the name of Yahweh, he shall surely be put to death; all the congregation shall certainly stone him: the foreigner as well as the native-born, when he blasphemes the Name, shall be put to death."
From Wikipedia, http://en.wikipedia.org/wiki/The_name_of_God_in_Judaism, "All

modern denominations of Judaism teach that the four letter name of God, YHVH, is forbidden to be uttered except by the High Priest, in the Temple. Since the Temple in Jerusalem is no longer extant, this name is never pronounced in religious rituals by Jews. Orthodox Jews never pronounce it for any reason. Some non-Orthodox Jews are willing to pronounce it, but for educational purposes only, and never in casual conversation or in prayer."

"....Before transcribing any of the divine names he [the scribe] prepares mentally to sanctify them. Once he begins a name he does not stop until it is finished, and he must not be interrupted while writing it, even to greet a king."

Deuteronomy 32:35-36: *"Vengeance is mine, and recompense, at the time when their foot slides; for the day of their calamity is at hand. The things that are to come on them shall make haste. For Yahweh will judge his people, and have compassion on his servants ...."*

Orb

A single, sunlit strand of spider silk,
shifting, lifting, on an autumn breeze -

> I remember when your words entangled
> my thoughts in webs of fear, and thrilling
> vibrations thrummed down those shimmering threads
> stretched tight across my sight, my path of flight.
>
> I remember when thoughts of you entangled
> my words. My speech, sure, slick and thrilling
> in soft, shuttered air, frayed into threads
> of breathless feeling, stilling dreams of flight.

perhaps a piece of broken web, used silk
trimmed and set to drift on a cooling breeze.

An Invitation

Three lines tonight - the first in many weeks.
An idle trip from mind to keys to screen
without a plan or map, or place to end,
but I pretend I saw them coming, felt
the urge, the Muse's touch, inhaled her scent.

Pretense, of course, but then, what else is new?
To tempt the temptress, fantasy or not,
to draw the coy seductress' sloe-eyed glance,
I beckon with a line, or two or three.
A tithe of sorts, an offering, a pledge,

of which she has no want, or need from me.
I see seduction as a pas de deux,
performance art at best, at worst an act.
But passion also needs a place to start.
It springs from want, or need, or dance.

Summer Night

the tree
swept together
earth air and light
cradled my past in leaves and limbs
tonight these fresh cut chips are all that remain

life is change still I look up expecting
refuge in now absent branches
not this accelerating
sweep of crystal
black

starlight
set in a vast
intoxicating dome
of ever expanding cosmic arms
inviting ancient fears and undreamt futures

gone are roots and trunk and embracing boughs
surprised and lost this summer night
my scattered thoughts
rise up released
and free

Sendai
12 March 2011

Dawn swells here, along earth's dark slow curve,
muted and distant, unraveling hope. A woman
squats, wet cheeks reflecting this intrusive light.
God, she thinks, is a trick of the mind, a priestly
sleight of hand to veil her broken world,
like incense burned to cover the stench of death.

Silence. Morning glances off splintered glass,
cold as the corpses that litter the long shoreline.
Nothing remains but shards of a hermit's bowl,
shattered like the rest of her world. She feels
betrayed, she screams for time to be stilled, reversed,
her life be given back, so she might die

as if the present did not exist, without
this pain, this loss, this struggle to live again.
A land laid waste in the rising sun stretches
the soul to its breaking point, scars the heart,
requires rejection of old beliefs, submission
to what cannot be changed except through change.

Her future lies lost, buried in splinters and mud,
yet to be found, yet to be marked. She mourns
and kneels before her grief as shadows retreat.
She stares but cannot see beyond these shards.
Tears rise in the early spring breeze. Shivering,
she lets the past slip from her hand.

Sonata for Moonlight and Shadows

Melancholy nocturne, sonata for moonlight,
shadows, and solitary dark wine nights.
Introit and reflection - a soft *sospirando*
dirge for the day used, laid waste and gone -
prologue to evening chill intrudes, invites.

Capricious memories, memetic rhythms
that don't exist, cannot be found in fact,
litter our pensive paths, shuffle past.
There, shards of dreams trip the light - fantastic,
quick glance, gleam and gone - a fancy fleeing.

We close and dance, awkward in soft cold light.
Crescendo, diminuendo, entangled medley
of shaded sky and spinning clouds of stars.
A muted wind stumbles past faintly
leaves to usher in a diva moon.

Across lost sheets, through half drawn curtains,
an ancient accolade, rising descant
and paean to passion finds its orchestral voice.
Naked, I embrace your sigh *fermata*
and shivering touch, *tremolo, coda*.

HAIKU

A Comment on Haiku:

Haiku is a rather specialized form of poetry, and arguably one that is better suited to the Japanese language than English. The more traditional structure of haiku consists of three lines using five syllables in the first and third lines, and seven in the second. A seasonal word or reference is almost mandatory, and haiku typically avoids reference to anything that is not 'of nature.' Excess words are avoided where possible, relying on the reader's ability to make reasonable assumptions based on their experiences and context.

More recently the form has loosened up and haiku using a 3-5-3 syllable format is now fairly common (actually better suited to English), along with variants with only two lines, and a somewhat grudging acceptance of haiku dealing with non-traditional topics and themes. Nevertheless haiku is still best seen as an effort to capture the distilled essence of the poem's subject matter in as minimalist a fashion as possible, following a rather stringent set of rules.

Frankly, my haiku plays rather fast and loose with the traditional approach, and many may not 'qualify' as haiku at all to a purist. Generally, my attempt has been to use the form as a highly compressed way to store thoughts and events, and as an exercise in 'distilling essence' as noted above.

Haiku in **bold** have previously been published (varying dates) in the Asahi Haikuist Network section (edited by David McMurray) of the online Asahi Shimbun.

Dawn arrives,
Slips between warm sheets.
Icy feet!

                    The hoped for
                    New Year has arrived.
                    I wonder.

Shush now, hush.
Fresh snow on old paths -
A new year.

                    After all, spring.
                    Here beside cold grave
                    A warm wind.

Fading dreams -
winds slip out, the door
gently closed.

                    Crossing days
                    chasing endless wind,
                    moon, and sun.

Chill autumn whispers
Answers to questions not asked.
Weeping winds depart.

                                    New green shoots
                                    Trembling urgent winds
                                    Morning sigh

Ah ...
Sugar water:
Bees porridge, cold.

                                    Ides of March
                                    Blustery winds chill
                                    Creaking bones

Crescent moon
Slicing through the cold
Scimitar

                                    Barking dogs
                                    Endings, beginnings
                                    Midnight moon

Awakened -
Not by sense, but sensed -
Rising winds

                I speak my fears
                You hear your anger
                It's done

Clouds gather
Ripples cross the pond
Angry words

                Summer rain
                Winter sun
                Love's caress

Poetry
Glossing over life
Mostly

                Haiku
                Life's insight
                Out

Boisterous, loud,
Nature's spring children
Mynahs chat

                    Summer gold
                    Tight skin glowing sun
                    Waikiki

Malibu
Sun glasses, tight skin
Golden state

                    Pulling weeds
                    Grumbling to myself
                    So Fruitless

Baby cries
Morning, noon, then night
Old man sighs

                    Reflecting
                    My voice, my values
                    Dad's mirror

One leaf moves
Green on white fencing
Chameleon

                        Sunlight gleams
                        Brilliant after rain
                        Dripping eaves

Dazzling
Gold, green, white on blue
Spring dances

                        Juices run
                        Lips, tongue, silken throat
                        Plump peaches

Spring morning
Shadows climb the fence
Coffee cools

                        Clouds, briefly
                        Then returning sun
                        Mother smiles

Twenty-one
All grown up, but still
Daddy's girl

                          Godot comes
                          Like my contractor
                          Half-built room

Still warm night
After cool showers
"?" "No."

                          Three hundred!
                          Bride and Groom's relief -
                          Parents pay

Summer night
Clothes, sheets, entangled
Disarrayed

                          Every night
                          Between slick covers
                          New lovers

Spider web
Laundry room corner
Spin cycle

                    Rose petals
                    Boutonnieres, nosegays
                    Love flowers

Epigrams
Haiku may be best
Maybe not

                    Your breathing
                    Warms my dreams; your breasts
                    Gentle rise, fall.

Sun rising
Eaglet spreads his wings
Son rising

                    Child woman:
                    Dragon parts the mists -
                    Sound alarms!

Silence, please!
Wind, birds, gravel walk,
Pounding head.

                City hick
                Sewing country quilts
                Camouflage

Abacus
Beads on bamboo rods
Past counting

                Web spinner
                Captured dreams struggle
                Summer love

spin, scatter
colors shimmer, fade
autumn leaves

                Arrayed against hope
                Ads, signs, half-truths, lies
                Candidates talking

I close the windows
paper and pencil are left
words - creation's tools

                    Thunderstorms,
                    Lightning bolts, and bombs -
                    Winter comes.

Mostly clouds
Dating service - free
Chance of snow

                    Half the time
                    Half truths seem to work
                    Elections

Threats, lies, twisted truths
Cultivating ignorance
Political ads

                    Sandcastle
                    On a winter beach
                    Changing tide

Dodging leaves
Red Cardinal flash
Aflutter

                      geckos form a line
                      along my light framed window
                      cafeteria

gecko sings
outside the screen, bugs
don't listen

                      God is found
                      along this river
                      flowing words

winding stream
too soon a river
to the sea

                      too soon this
                      haiku ends too soon
                      this haiku

www.ingramcontent.com/pod-product-compliance
Lightning Source LLC
Chambersburg PA
CBHW031436040426
42444CB00006B/841